PLANTING the WILD GARDEN

To Pat Leuchtman, dear friend and gardener extraordinaire.
And once again to Steve, my favorite gentleman farmer.

—K. O. G.

To Liberty Hyde Bailey, a very famous scientist who studied and
gathered plants from around the world. He wanted
children to look carefully at plants and trees and ask
questions. He wanted children to write
those questions down in their nature journals.
Can you ask questions about the seeds on the endpapers?

—W. A. H.

Published by
PEACHTREE PUBLISHERS
1700 Chattahoochee Avenue
Atlanta, Georgia 30318-2112
www.peachtree-online.com

Text © 2011 by Kathryn O. Galbraith
Illustrations © 2011 by Wendy Anderson Halperin

First trade paperback edition published in 2013

Art direction by Loraine M. Joyner
Typesetting by Melanie McMahon Ives

Illustrations created in pencil and watercolor on 100% rag, archival watercolor paper; text typeset in International Typeface Corporation's Leawood Book by Les Usherwood and Stone Sans by Sumner Stone and John Renner; title typeset in ITC's Belwe Light by Georg Belwe.

Printed in November 2015 by Imago in Singapore
10 9 8 7 6 5 (hardcover)
10 9 8 7 6 5 4 3 2 (trade paperback)

Library of Congress Cataloging-in-Publication Data
Galbraith, Kathryn Osebold.
  Planting the wild garden / written by Kathryn O. Galbraith; illustrated by Wendy Anderson Halperin.
      p. cm.
  ISBN 978-1-56145-563-8 (hardcover)
  ISBN 978-1-56145-791-5 (trade paperback)
  1. Seeds—Dispersal—Juvenile literature. I. Halperin, Wendy Anderson. II. Title.
QK929.G35 2011
581.4'67--dc22
                                          2010026898

PLANTING the WILD GARDEN

Written by
Kathryn O. Galbraith

Illustrated by
Wendy Anderson Halperin

PEACHTREE
ATLANTA

The farmer and her boy plant their garden. They drop seeds—tiny, fat, round, and oval—into the earth. From these seeds, pumpkins and peas, carrots and cabbages will grow.

In the wild meadow garden, many seeds
are planted too, but not by farmers' hands.

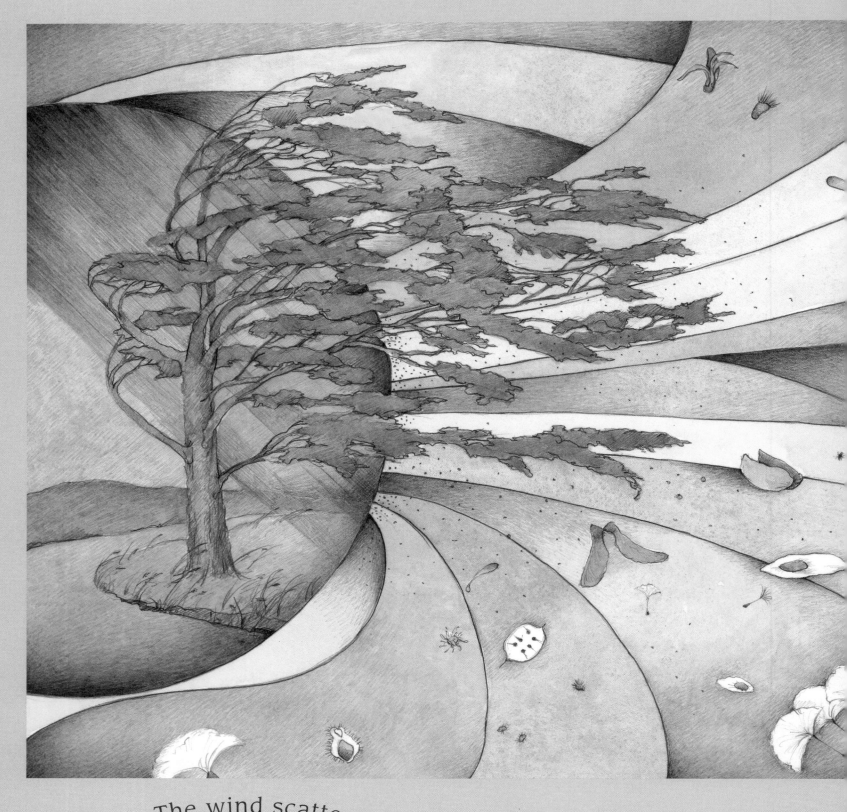

The wind scatters seeds. It spills them. And spins them.

Ooooooo—whishhh!

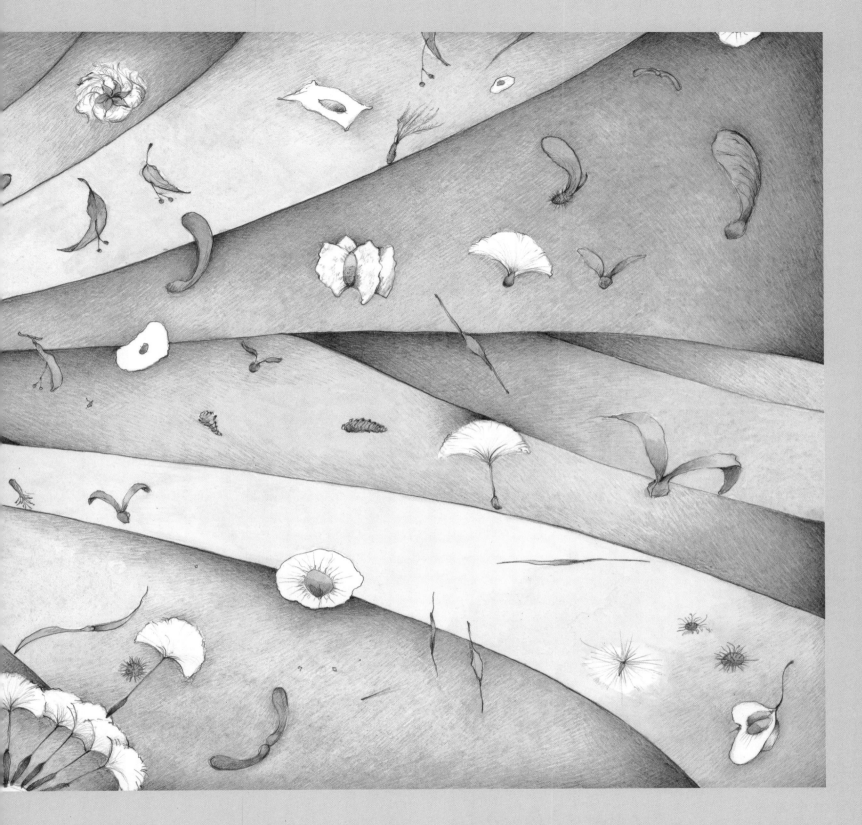

And sweeps them up, up into the sunlight and out across the fields.

Per-chik-o-ree! Per-chik-o-ree!

Waves of black and gold dip into the meadow.

Peck. Peck. Peck.

The flock of goldfinches bobbles and sways.
Some thistle seeds float to the earth. Others
are strewn across the meadow in droppings.

Under the afternoon sun, the pods of the Scotch broom grow hot and dry. **Snap!** Out pop their seeds, like popcorn from a pan. **Snap!**

They land here. And there. And **snap!** over there, where they will have more room to grow.

Plip-plop! The rain patters on dusty leaves.

Raindrops splash and splatter the dry earth,
washing seeds to new places in the meadow.

The stream carries seeds too.

Gulp! Gulp! Minnows dine on some.

Others lodge along the bank. Next spring new
pussy willow shoots will poke up through the mud.

Hidden in the tall weeds, a rabbit nibbles
a stalk of yarrow. Now a nibble of grass.

Nibble, **Hop,**
nibble. **hop.** Another seed falls to the ground.

A hungry shadow watches.

She slips past the tangle of cockleburs.

She creeps through the Queen Anne's lace.

Seeds catch on her thick coat.

They hook onto her white-tipped tail and—

JUMP!

—fly off everywhere!

In the summer moonlight, one...two...three...four masked faces, four ringed tails. A family of raccoons feasts on blackberries.

Chomp.   **Chomp.**
Chomp.

When they amble home again, bits of berries and seeds go with them. Next spring, new prickly canes will pop up everywhere.

Thump, bump. An acorn falls. Then another.

Quick! The squirrel buries both and hunts for more.
Quick!

When winter comes, **scratch,** scratch. **Scratch.**
Down through the snow he digs. One fat acorn.
Then another. Plenty of food to last 'til spring.

Some nuts are lost, but few are wasted. This great oak tree grew from an acorn buried many years ago.

Stomp! *Stomp!* People help plant the meadow too.
Seeds travel on muddy boots.

Hitchhike on sweaters. Snag on socks.
And **whoosh!** Sail on a puff of breath.

Seed by seed, we planted this wild meadow garden.
Wind and water. Birds and animals. Plants and people.

All of us.

Together.

Bibliography

These are a few of the many books that I found helpful in developing the text for PLANTING THE WILD GARDEN:

BERRIES, NUTS AND SEEDS by Diane L. Burns, illustrated by John F. McGee (NorthWord)

FAMILIAR GARDEN BIRDS OF AMERICA: AN ILLUSTRATED GUIDE TO THE BIRDS IN YOUR OWN BACKYARD by Henry H. Collins Jr. and Ned R. Boyajian, illustrated by John C. Yrizarry and Nina Williams (HarperCollins)

A FIELD GUIDE TO WESTERN BIRDS by Roger Tory Peterson (Houghton Mifflin)

FLOWERS, FRUITS AND SEEDS by Angela Royston (Heinemann)

THE HIDDEN MAGIC OF SEEDS by Dorothy Edwards Shuttlesworth (Rodale)

HOW PLANTS TRAVEL by Joan Elma Rahn, illustrated by Ginny Linville Winter (Atheneum)

HOW SEEDS TRAVEL by Cynthia Overbeck Bix, photographs by Shabo Hani (Lerner)

NATIONAL GEOGRAPHIC FIELD GUIDE TO THE BIRDS OF NORTH AMERICA edited by Jon L. Dunn and Jonathan Alderfer (National Geographic Society)

PLANTS ON THE GO: A BOOK ABOUT SEED DISPERSAL by Eleanor B. Heady, illustrated by Susan Swann (Parents' Magazine)

RIDE THE WIND: AIRBORNE JOURNEYS OF ANIMALS AND PLANTS by Seymour Simon, illustrated by Elsa Warnick (Browndeer)

SEEDS AND WEEDS by Rena K. Kirkpatrick, illustrated by Debbie King (Raintree Steck-Vaughn)

SEEDS BY WIND AND WATER by Helene J. Jordan, illustrated by Nils Hogner (Thomas Y. Crowell Company)

SEEDS POP, STICK, GLIDE by Patricia Lauber, photographs by Jerome Wexler (Knopf)